terrific table toppers
with Patrick Lose

DECORATE YOUR HOME WITH FAST FUSIBLE APPLIQUÉ ■ **10 QUILT PROJECTS**

C&T PUBLISHING

Text copyright © 2009 by Patrick Lose

Artwork copyright © 2009 by C&T Publishing, Inc.

Publisher: Amy Marson

Creative Director: Gailen Runge

Acquisitions Editor: Susanne Woods

Editor: Cynthia Bix

Technical Editors: Sandy Peterson and Teresa Stroin

Copyeditor/Proofreader: Wordfirm Inc.

Cover Designer: Kristen Yenche

Book Designer: Kerry Graham

Production Coordinators: Kirstie L. Pettersen and Casey Dukes

Illustrators: Patrick Lose and Kirstie L. Pettersen

Photography by Christina Carty-Francis and Diane Pedersen of C&T Publishing, Inc., unless otherwise noted.

Published by C&T Publishing, Inc., P.O. Box 1456, Lafayette, CA 94549

Library of Congress Cataloging-in-Publication Data

Lose, Patrick.

Terrific table toppers with Patrick Lose : decorate your home with fast fusible appliqué : 10 quilt projects / Patrick Michael Lose.

p. cm.

ISBN 978-1-57120-845-3 (soft cover)

1. Appliqué–Patterns. 2. Tablecloths. I. Title.

TT779.L677 2009

746.44'5041–dc22

2009013023

Printed in China

10 9 8 7 6 5 4 3 2 1

acknowledgments

For their friendship and assistance with the projects in this book, I would like to thank the following:

Faith Kalbeck

Hope Kalbeck

Gary Rushton

Mary McElvain

Brenda Moseley

Joan May

Joan Witt

dedication

To my granddaughters, Lauryn and Lily, with all my love.

contents

PROJECTS

introduction

Place mats and table runners are fun to make and, because they're also easy to put together in no time at all, they're the perfect project to turn to when time is hard to come by. I've never heard of a quilter who doesn't have a stash pile, and the projects you'll find in this book will put it to good use.

My friends and I got together and had a great time making these table toppers. Whether you make them on your own or invite a group of your friends to do the same, I hope you have a lot of fun, too!

Cheers,

Patrick

general instructions

As tempting as it may be to jump right into your project, read the instructions thoroughly before you begin working.

The table runners and place mats in this book are constructed in the same way you would make a small quilt. You create a quilt top, layer it with batting and backing, and then quilt and bind it.

Projects are pieced using a ¼″-wide seam allowance, with the fabrics placed right sides together. Most are appliquéd using a fusible method (page 7). A blind-stitch appliqué method is used for the *Urban Vibe* project (page 25).

TOOLS

Make sure you have all the necessary tools at hand before you start working. Following is a list of helpful tools that will make your stitching easier.

▪ Rotary cutter and cutting mat

▪ Transparent acrylic gridded ruler

▪ Sewing machine in good working order, capable of doing a narrow zigzag or satin stitch

▪ Paper scissors

▪ Fabric scissors

▪ Sewing machine needles, size 80/12 universal. Titanium needles are great but not necessary. A number 12, 14, or 16 topstitching needle works best for satin stitching the fused appliqués. A 60/8 universal needle is used for the blind-stitch appliqué technique used in *Urban Vibe* (page 25).

▪ Various threads for appliqué and quilting

▪ Iron and ironing board

▪ Darning or stippling foot for free-motion quilting

▪ Open-toe or appliqué foot for satin stitching and for the blind-stitch appliqué technique used in *Urban Vibe* (page 25)

▪ Safety pins

▪ Fusible web (Lite Steam-A-Seam 2)

▪ Freezer paper used for the blind-stitch appliqué technique in *Urban Vibe* (page 25)

▪ Lightbox for transferring pattern placement lines (optional)

FABRICS

Making place mats and table runners is a great way to use fat quarters that you have stashed away. These treasures can be the background or backing of a place mat or can be pieced to make a runner, and they don't even have to match each other. Additionally, they can be cut and appliquéd onto your creations. Use your imagination!

I don't prewash my fabrics for quilting. This is my personal preference, and I've never had a problem with colors bleeding. If I do wash the finished piece, the minimal shrinkage creates a slightly puckered quilt with a softer look and feel. Some people always prewash, and that's perfectly fine. Just be sure that if you prewash, you use warm water to allow the fabric to shrink as much as it's going to. Tumble dry the fabric, and remove it from the dryer when it's still slightly damp. Always iron the fabric before measuring and cutting. Do not use starch on fabrics that will be used for appliqué pieces. It could make the fabric difficult to fuse.

It's extremely important to measure and cut your fabrics accurately and to stitch using an exact ¼″ seam allowance. I'm certain you'll be proud of your finished piece if you follow these simple rules.

NOTE: The usable fabric width for these projects is assumed to be 42″ wide.

SPECIAL NOTE

All of the place mat projects in this book call for enough fabric to make a pair. You'll most likely want to make more than one, and making a pair is a more economical use of your fabric if you're purchasing fabric especially for this project. Also, a set of two or four place mats makes a much better gift than a single one!

Off the Table

I originally designed the table runners in this book to be used on dining tables and sideboards, but why not use your imagination to find other purposes for them around the house?

What about making a bed scarf from the *Make a Wish* birthday runner and placing it across the foot of your child's bed on his or her birthday? Or how about using my *Morning Coffee* runner on—where else?—your coffee table.

Maybe you could create a door banner or a wall-hanging by simply making a half runner and adding a hanging sleeve.

The possibilities are endless!

Here's *Make a Wish* (page 21) as it would look made into a door banner.

APPLIQUÉ

Most of the appliqué projects in this book use a fused method. I've used satin stitching to finish the raw edges of the appliqués in these projects, but feel free to appliqué using your favorite method. Should you wish to do hand appliqué (knock yourself out!), you'll need to trace the printed patterns in mirror image and add seam allowances to them. Then you can lay them onto the right side of the fabric for cutting. The blind-stitch appliqué method is used for *Urban Vibe* (page 25).

fusible appliqué preparations

Template patterns are printed actual size and are reversed for tracing onto paper-backed fusible web. Be sure to use a lightweight, paper-backed fusible web that is suitable for sewing. I use Lite Steam-A-Seam 2, because I like the body and stability it gives to pieces like the ones in this book.

1. Lay the fusible web, paper side up, over each pattern piece, and trace the shape onto the paper side. Leave approximately ¼″ of cutting space around each traced piece (a total of ½″ between pieces). Trace as many as indicated by the number on each pattern. It helps to write the name, piece number, and fabric color on each piece as you trace it.

NOTE: In places where the pieces butt one another, overlapping them helps to keep them from gapping. Cut the pieces to size, and then, when appliquéing, overlap by a hair.

2. Use paper-cutting scissors to roughly cut all of the pieces approximately ¼″ outside the traced lines.

3. Following the manufacturer's instructions for the fusible web, fuse the traced pattern pieces, paper side up, onto the wrong side of the fabric you've chosen for your appliqués.

4. Cut out the pieces neatly along the traced lines.

5. Transfer any placement and stitching lines to the right side of the fabric using a lightbox and a pencil.

6. Arrange all of the appliqués as pictured in the project, and when you're satisfied with the arrangement, fuse them to the background.

LAYERING AND QUILTING

I like to use a single layer of thin cotton batting such as Warm & Natural because of its stability and body. It's especially nice to have this stability in projects like these place mats and runners. If possible, cut your backing fabric and batting to measure an inch or so larger than your quilt top on all sides. Sandwich the batting between the quilt top and the backing, wrong sides together, and pin through all the layers, several inches apart, smoothing the quilt top outward from the center.

TIP

You can also iron fusible web to the wrong sides of some of the scrap fabrics in your stash and cut them as desired to make small pieces for projects that don't require patterns, such as the confetti pieces in *Party Pizzazz* on **page 17.**

All the quilting in this book was done by machine. For free-motion or meander quilting, I use a darning or stippling foot and lower the feed dogs on my machine. Quilt as desired, or refer to the photos and quilting suggestions that are included with the projects.

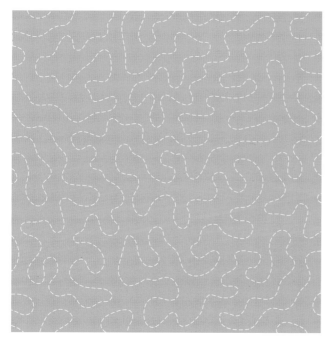

Example of free-motion quilting

After you have finished quilting, square up the sides of your table topper, and trim any excess fabric and batting.

SATIN STITCHING

When I outline the fusible appliqué pieces with satin stitching, I machine satin stitch after the projects are layered and quilted, just before the binding is added. This is my "fast and much easier" way of doing these projects. Having the quilting finished before the satin stitching is done stabilizes the piece and makes it easier to satin stitch. It also leaves out the unnecessary (and more costly) step of using a stabilizer and having to restitch around the appliqués.

If you're new to satin stitching, be sure to practice stitching on layered scraps first, adjusting your stitch width and length until you get the look you desire. I also look at the layering of the appliquéd pieces, and I try to stitch around the uppermost layers last. That way, the ends of the "underneath" stitching lines are covered by a continuous line of stitching on top.

Backing Hints

The quilt top backgrounds for most of the table runners in this book are cut selvage to selvage. The backing pieces are also cut selvage to selvage, but because you want your backing to be a little larger than the quilt top, you'll need to piece an inset into the center of the backing to lengthen it. To accomplish this, cut your backing the width required in the pattern, and from selvage to selvage. Then cut a coordinating fabric into a block that measures 6˝ by the width (the smaller dimension) of the runner backing. Fold the backing in half, aligning the short sides. Crease or press the centered fold line. Cut along this crease, and insert the inset block using ¼˝ seams with the fabrics right sides together. The inset is the perfect place to use a permanent fabric marker to add your signature and the date you created your masterpiece!

BINDING

The instructions for each project give you the amount of binding necessary to finish your table topper project.

1. Cut 2½˝-wide strips selvage to selvage, using a rotary cutter, a mat, and a transparent acrylic gridded ruler. These strips will measure 40˝–44˝ long, after you have straightened your fabric and cut off the selvages.

2. Right sides together, use diagonal seams to join the binding strips. Trim the seam allowances, and press the seams open.

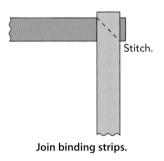

Join binding strips.

3. Fold one end of the strip at a 45° angle to create a point. Press. Fold the binding strip in half lengthwise with the wrong sides together and the long raw edges aligned. Press.

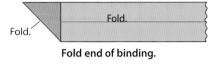

Fold end of binding.

Fold binding lengthwise.

4. Place the folded binding strip on one edge of the quilt top, aligning the raw edges of the quilt and the binding. Stitch through all the layers using a ¼˝ seam allowance. Stop stitching ¼˝ from the corner. Pivot and stitch a diagonal line to the corner as shown below. Backstitch at least 2 stitches, remove the quilt from the machine, and clip the threads.

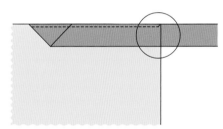

Stop stitching ¼˝ from corner, pivot, and stitch.

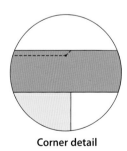

Corner detail

5. Fold up the binding, and finger crease the fold.

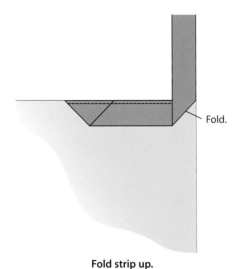

Fold.

Fold strip up.

6. Holding the creased fold in place, fold the binding down and align the raw edges with the next side of the quilt. Start stitching again at the corner, through all the layers. Stitch around the entire runner or place mat, treating each corner as you did the first.

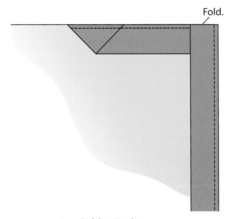

Fold.

Fold strip down.

7. When you return to where you started, stitch the binding past the second angled fold about ½˝. Backstitch at least 2 stitches, and clip the threads. Cut off the excess binding.

8. Turn the binding to the back over the quilt edge, aligning the fold of the binding with the machine stitching you just finished.

9. Sew the binding onto the backing. You can do this by machine, from the front, or by hand. In either case, miter the corners on the back side of the quilt also. If you choose to stitch the binding to the back by machine, lap the fold over the seamline used to attach the binding to the front. Then stitch as close to the binding seam as possible from the front, catching the overlapped binding fold on the back. If I miss a spot or two, I just finish it off by hand. Besides, if your dinner guests are inspecting the underside of your table decorations, you might want to reconsider their inclusion on your guest lists (*wink*)!

Urban Vibe (page 25)

Morning
Coffee

Here's a table topper for those who like to piece as well as appliqué. Show it off the next time you have company for coffee!

Finished size: 16½˝ × 44½˝

Table runner made by Brenda Moseley, Gary Rushton, and Patrick

FABRIC AND SUPPLIES

Note: A 42˝ available width of fabric is assumed.

Green: 1¼ yards for background, backing, and binding

Gold: ¼ yard for pieced border and star appliqués

Red: ¼ yard for pieced border and heart appliqués

Brown: ½ yard for pieced border and cup appliqués

Batting: 18˝ × 46˝

Fusible web (18˝ wide): ½ yard

CUTTING FABRICS

From Green

The center panel is cut after the borders are assembled (see Center Panel, page 13).

Cut 1 rectangle 18˝ × width of fabric for the backing. Remove the selvages.*

Cut 4 strips 2½˝ × width of fabric for the binding.

* Cut the backing in half, and add a coordinating inset to the backing as desired to make it larger than the runner top (see Backing Hints, page 8).

From Gold:
Cut 2 strips 1½˝ × width of fabric for the pieced border.

From Red:
Cut 2 strips 1½˝ × width of fabric for the pieced border.

From Brown:
Cut 4 strips 1½˝ × width of fabric for the pieced border.

MAKING THE BORDERS

1. Sew 1 brown strip to 1 gold strip. Press toward the brown strip. Make 2. Crosscut sewn strips into 56 segments that are 1½˝ wide.

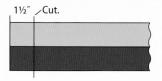

2. Sew pairs of the segments together in 4-patch units, alternating color placement as shown, to make 28 of Unit A. Be careful to match center seams.

Unit A

3. Sew 1 brown strip to 1 red strip. Press toward the brown strip. Make 2. As in Step 1, cut the sewn strips into 56 segments that are 1½˝ wide.

4. Sew pairs of the segments together in 4-patch units, alternating color placement as shown, to make 28 of Unit B. Be careful to match center seams.

Unit B

5. Using 10 Unit A's alternating with 10 Unit B's, make a side border, keeping the color orientation as shown. Be careful to match center seams as you add units. Make 2.

Unit A   Unit B

Make 2 side borders.

6. Using 4 Unit A's alternating with 4 Unit B's, make a top border, keeping the color orientation as shown. Be careful to match center seams. Make 2.

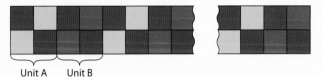

Make top and bottom border.

CENTER PANEL

1. Measure the length of the 2 side borders (including the 2 end seam allowances), and take the average.

2. Measure the length of the 2 top borders, excluding both end 4-patch units, and take the average. Add ½˝ to this length for the seam allowances.

3. Cut the green rectangular center panel to the dimensions measured in Steps 1 and 2. Your dimensions should be 12½˝ × 40½˝, or thereabouts. Be sure to remove the selvages before cutting the panel dimensions.

CREATING THE APPLIQUÉS

All the appliqué template patterns are in the pullout section. They are printed actual size and are reversed for tracing onto fusible web.

Trace the heart-shaped sections from the brown cup fabric by following the solid line shown on the pattern. Cut the red hearts roughly ⅛˝ larger than the pattern on all sides, and place them over the cut out section of the brown cups.

Refer to Fusible Appliqué Preparations, page 7, for additional instructions on creating the appliqués.

POSITIONING AND FUSING THE APPLIQUÉS

1. Remove the paper backing from the appliqués.

2. Refer to the project photo (page 11) and the illustration (page 14) for placement. Arrange the appliqués on the background, allowing room for the curly steam satin stitching. Place the red hearts over the cutout sections of the brown cups so there is no gap between them. Be sure to place the fusible side of the fabric against the background. Finger-press the appliqués into place. Remember that there is a ¼˝-wide seam allowance for the borders on all sides of the center panel, so don't place anything there.

3. When you're satisfied with the arrangement of all of the appliqué pieces, fuse them into place on the center panel, following the manufacturer's instructions for the fusible web you're using.

ASSEMBLING THE RUNNER TOP

1. Sew the side borders onto the center panel, keeping the orientation of the border squares as shown in the illustration on page 14. Press the seam allowances toward the borders.

2. Sew the top and bottom borders onto the center panel. Be careful to match the seams of the squares in the corners of the borders. Press.

QUILTING AND FINISHING

Refer to Layering and Quilting (page 7), Satin Stitching (page 8), and Binding (page 9).

1. Sandwich the batting between the runner top and backing, wrong sides together, smoothing the top outward from the center. Pin the layers together.

2. Quilt as desired. I used pale yellow thread in a meandering quilting pattern across the whole runner top.

3. Add satin stitching around the appliqués. I used black thread to outline them and make them pop. Note that the designs for satin stitching the curly steam patterns shown in the pullout are **not reversed** and may be stitched as shown. Use your favorite method to transfer those designs to the runner top.

4. Bind the runner.

Flower
Power

Inspired by brightly colored Hawaiian shirts and all of the tropical paradise daydreams that go along with them, these place mats are fun to make and have around when you can't actually get away to the islands.

Finished size: 14″ × 18″

Place mats made and quilted by Patrick

FABRIC AND SUPPLIES

Note: A 42˝ available width of fabric is assumed.

To make 2 place mats, 1 red and 1 blue:

Blue: ½ yard or 2 fat quarters for background and backing

Red: ½ yard or 2 fat quarters for background and backing

White: ¾ yard for hibiscus appliqués and binding

Batting: 2 pieces, each 16˝ × 20˝

Fusible web (18˝ wide): ¾ yard

CUTTING FABRICS

From Blue:
Cut 1 rectangle 14˝ × 18˝ for the background.

Cut 1 rectangle 16˝ × 20˝ for the backing.

From Red:
Cut 1 rectangle 14˝ × 18˝ for the background.

Cut 1 rectangle 16˝ × 20˝ for the backing.

From White:
Cut 4 strips 2½˝ × width of fabric for the binding.

CREATING THE APPLIQUÉS

All the appliqué template patterns are in the pullout section. They are printed actual size and are reversed for tracing onto fusible web.

Refer to Fusible Appliqué Preparations (page 7) for instructions on creating the appliqués.

POSITIONING AND FUSING THE APPLIQUÉS

1. Remove the paper backing from the appliqués.

2. Refer to the project photo (page 15) and illustration to the right for placement. Arrange the appliqués on the background fabric. Be sure to place the fusible side of the fabric against the background. Finger-press the appliqués into place. Remember that there is a ¼˝-wide seam allowance on all sides of the background for the binding. The bottom and left sides of the hibiscus template extend into this seam allowance.

3. When you're satisfied with the arrangement of the appliqué pieces, fuse them into place on the background, following the manufacturer's instructions for the fusible web you're using.

QUILTING AND FINISHING

Refer to Layering and Quilting (page 7), Satin Stitching (page 8), and Binding (page 9).

1. Sandwich the batting between the place mat tops and their backings, wrong sides together, smoothing the tops outward from the center. Pin the layers together.

2. Quilt as desired. I used white thread in a loose, meandering pattern like that shown in Layering and Quilting (page 8) over the whole place mat, including the appliqués.

3. I satin stitched around the edges of the hibiscus flowers using white thread with a very narrow stitch, set at a 1.5 width. This makes it easier to stitch the corners and curves, and the white on white helps to hide a lot of sins in your stitching!

4. Bind the place mats.

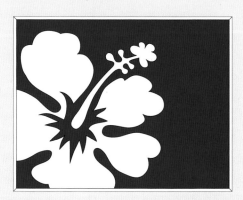

Party Pizzazz

Colorful balloons, confetti, and falling stars create a centerpiece for any occasion that calls for a celebration.

Finished size: approximately 14˝ × 42˝

Table runner made by Joan May and finished by Gary Rushton and Patrick

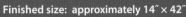

FABRIC AND SUPPLIES

Note: A 42″ available width of fabric is assumed.

Black: 1 yard for background and backing

Gold: ¼ yard or 1 fat quarter for stars

Red: ¼ yard or 1 fat quarter for balloons and confetti

Blue: ¼ yard or 1 fat quarter for balloons and confetti

Yellow: ¼ yard or 1 fat quarter for balloons and confetti

Bright colored fabric: scraps for confetti

Purple: ⅜ yard for binding and confetti

Batting: 16″ × 44″

Fusible web (18″ wide): 1 yard

CUTTING FABRICS

From Black:

Cut 1 rectangle 14″ × width of fabric for the background. Remove the selvages.

Cut 1 rectangle 16″ × width of fabric for the backing. Remove the selvages.*

* Cut the backing in half, and add a coordinating inset to the backing as desired to make it larger than the background piece (see Backing Hints, page 8).

From Purple:

Cut 4 strips 2½″ × width of fabric for the binding.

CREATING THE APPLIQUÉS

All the appliqué template patterns are in the pullout section. They are printed actual size and are reversed for tracing onto fusible web.

Refer to Fusible Appliqué Preparations (page 7) for additional instructions on creating the appliqués.

POSITIONING AND FUSING THE APPLIQUÉS

1. Remove the paper backing from the appliqués.

2. Refer to the project photo (page 17) and the illustration at the right for placement. Arrange the star appliqués on the background, then the balloons, overlapping as desired. Then place the confetti in a pleasing pattern. Be sure to place the fusible side of the fabric against the background. Finger-press the appliqués into place. Remember that there is a ¼″-wide

seam allowance for binding on all sides of the background.

3. When you're satisfied with the arrangement of all of the appliqué pieces, fuse them into place on the background, following the manufacturer's instructions for the fusible web you're using.

QUILTING AND FINISHING

Refer to Layering and Quilting (page 7), Satin Stitching (page 8), and Binding (page 9).

1. Sandwich the batting between the runner top and backing, wrong sides together, smoothing the top outward from the center. Pin the layers together.

2. Quilt as desired. I used gold metallic thread in a loose, meandering pattern, like that shown in Layering and Quilting (page 8), over the whole place mat, including the appliqués.

3. Add satin stitching around the appliqué shapes using gold metallic thread. Satin stitch ″string lines″ from the balloons using the same thread, or improvise!

4. Bind the runner.

Lots of Love

Here's a bold graphic design to make for a romantic Valentine's Day dinner or anytime you'd like to give a heartwarming gift to a special someone.

Finished size: 14″ × 45½″

Table runner made by Gary Rushton and Patrick

FABRIC AND SUPPLIES

Note: A 42″ available width of fabric is assumed.

Ivory: ½ yard for background and half-heart appliqués

Merlot: 1⅜ yards for background, half-heart appliqués, binding, and backing

Batting: 16″ × 47″

Fusible web (18″ wide): ⅞ yard

CUTTING FABRICS

From Ivory:
Cut 3 rectangles 8″ × 14″ for the backgrounds.

From Merlot:
Cut 3 rectangles 8″ × 14″ for the backgrounds.

Cut 1 rectangle 16″ × width of fabric for the backing. Remove selvages.*

Cut 4 strips 2½″ × length of fabric for the binding.

* Cut the backing in half, and add a coordinating inset to the backing as desired to make it larger than the background piece (see Backing Hints, page 8).

CREATING THE APPLIQUÉS

All the appliqué template patterns are in the pullout section. They are printed actual size and are reversed for tracing onto fusible web.

Make a total of 6 ivory half hearts, flip the template, and make 6 merlot half hearts.

Refer to Fusible Appliqué Preparations (page 7) for additional instructions on creating the appliqués.

POSITIONING AND FUSING THE APPLIQUÉS

1. Remove the paper backing from the appliqués.

2. Refer to the project photo (page 19) and the block placement template (on the pullout) for placement. Arrange the appliqués on the block fabric, placing each half heart the same distance from the bottom edge as shown on the block placement template. Be sure to place the fusible side of the fabric against the background blocks. Finger-press the appliqués into place. Remember that there is a ¼″-wide seam allowance on all sides of the background blocks.

3. When you're satisfied with the arrangement of all of the appliqué pieces, fuse them into place on the blocks, following the manufacturer's instructions for the fusible web you're using.

ASSEMBLING THE RUNNER TOP

Refer to the project photo on page 19 and the illustration below, and stitch the 6 background blocks with the fused half-heart shapes together in a row. Be careful to match the heart points. Press the seams open.

QUILTING AND FINISHING

Refer to Layering and Quilting (page 7), Satin Stitching (page 8), and Binding (page 9).

1. Sandwich the batting between the runner top and backing, wrong sides together, smoothing the top outward from the center. Pin the layers together.

2. Quilt as desired. I used merlot-colored thread in a loose, meandering pattern, like that shown in Layering and Quilting (page 8), over the whole runner, including the appliqué.

3. I satin stitched around the curved edges of the half hearts using merlot-colored thread.

4. Bind the runner.

Make a Wish

Whether you make it as a gift or use it for all of the birthday celebrations in your family, this cupcake runner will make someone's day very special.

Finished size: 14˝ × 42˝

Table runner made by Gary Rushton and Patrick

FABRIC AND SUPPLIES

Note: A 42″ available width of fabric is assumed.

Blue: 1 yard for background and backing

Dark purple: 10″ × 12″ rectangle for cupcakes

Light purple: 6″ × 7″ rectangle for candles

White: ¼ yard or 1 fat quarter for frosting

Orange 1: 8″ × 9″ square for small and medium stars

Orange 2: ⅜ yard for small flames and binding

Yellow 1: 8″ × 14″ rectangle for large stars

Yellow 2: 6″ × 6″ square for large flames

Batting: 16″ × 44″

Fusible web (18″ wide): 1 yard

CUTTING FABRICS

From Blue:
Cut 1 rectangle 14″ × width of fabric for the background. Remove the selvages.

Cut 1 rectangle 16″ × width of fabric for the backing. Remove the selvages.*

*Cut the backing in half, and add a coordinating inset to the backing as desired to make it larger than the background piece (see Backing Hints, page 8).

From Orange 2:
Cut 4 strips 2½″ × width of fabric for the binding.

CREATING THE APPLIQUÉS

All the appliqué template patterns are in the pullout section. They are printed actual size and are reversed for tracing onto fusible web.

Refer to Fusible Appliqué Preparations, page 7, for additional instructions on creating the appliqués.

POSITIONING AND FUSING THE APPLIQUÉS

1. Remove the paper backing from the appliqués.

2. Refer to the project photo (page 21) and the illustration to the right for placement. Arrange the appliqués on the background, overlapping as desired. Be sure to place the fusible side of the fabric against the background. Finger-press the appliqués into place. Remember that there is a ¼″-wide seam allowance for binding on all sides of the background.

3. When you're satisfied with the arrangement of all of the appliqué pieces, fuse them into place on the background, following the manufacturer's instructions for the fusible web you're using.

QUILTING AND FINISHING

Refer to Layering and Quilting (page 7), Satin Stitching (page 8), and Binding (page 9).

1. Sandwich the batting between the runner top and backing, wrong sides together, smoothing the top outward from the center. Pin the layers together.

2. Quilt as desired. I used a loopy meandering path on the whole runner, including the appliqués.

3. Add satin stitching around the appliqués. I used several different thread colors that either blended with the appliqué or created a nice outline for them.

4. Bind the runner.

Fright Night

*A haunting harvest moon hangs
in the sky over this scary silhouette
scene that's frightfully simple to sew.*

Finished size: approximately 14″ × 42″

Table runner made by Joan Witt, Gary Rushton, and Patrick

FABRIC AND SUPPLIES

Note: A 42″ available width of fabric is assumed.

Violet: 1 yard for background and backing

Black: ⅞ yard for houses, bats, moon faces, and binding.

Orange: 16″ × 8″ rectangle for harvest moons

Yellow: 13″ × 8″ rectangle for stars and house windows.

Batting: 16″ × 44″

Fusible adhesive (18″ wide): 1 yard

CUTTING FABRICS

From Violet:

Cut 1 rectangle 14″ × width of fabric for the background. Remove the selvages.

Cut 1 rectangle 16″ × width of fabric for the backing. Remove the selvages.*

* Cut the backing in half, and add a coordinating inset to the backing as desired to make it larger than the background piece (see Backing Hints, page 8).

From Black:

Cut 4 strips 2½″ × width of fabric for the binding.

CREATING THE APPLIQUÉS

All the appliqué template patterns are in the pullout section. They are printed actual size and are reversed for tracing onto fusible web.

Cut the yellow windows roughly ⅛″ larger than the templates on all sides, and place them under the cutout sections of the houses.

Refer to Fusible Appliqué Preparations, page 7, for additional instructions on creating the appliqués.

POSITIONING AND FUSING THE APPLIQUÉS

1. Remove the paper backing from the appliqués.

2. Refer to the project photo (page 23) and the illustration to the right for placement. Arrange the appliqués on the background, overlapping as desired. Place the yellow windows underneath the house cutouts so that there is no gap between pieces. Be sure to place the fusible side of the fabric against the background. Finger-press the appliqués into place. Remember that there is a ¼″-wide seam allowance for binding on all sides of the background. The bottom and one side of each house extend into this seam allowance.

3. When you're satisfied with the arrangement of all of the appliqué pieces, fuse them into place on the background, following the manufacturer's instructions for the fusible web you're using.

QUILTING AND FINISHING

Refer to Layering and Quilting (page 7), Satin Stitching (page 8), and Binding (page 9).

1. Sandwich the batting between the runner top and backing, wrong sides together, smoothing the top outward from the center. Pin the layers together.

2. Quilt as desired. I used a horizontal meandering stitch pattern in black across the whole runner.

3. I satin stitched with black thread around the outline of each appliqué piece and added extra details for the house railings and tombstone crosses.

4. Bind the runner.

urban vibe

Two coordinating place mats can be alternated on the same table with this earthy-colored runner, using one fabric print in several colors for a sophisticated, contemporary look.

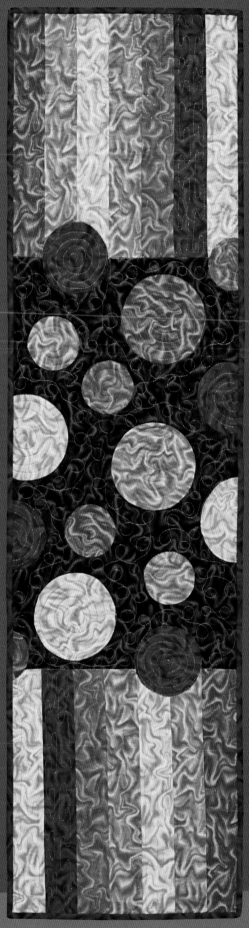

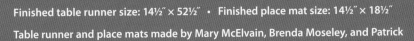

Finished table runner size: 14½˝ × 52½˝   •   **Finished place mat size:** 14½˝ × 18½˝

Table runner and place mats made by Mary McElvain, Brenda Moseley, and Patrick

table runner

FABRIC AND SUPPLIES

Note: A 42˝ available width of fabric is assumed.

Caramel: 1 yard for stripes, appliqués, and backing

Chocolate: ½ yard for top background

Merlot: ⅝ yard for stripes, appliqués, and binding

Moss: 1 fat quarter for stripes and appliqués

Corn Silk: 1 fat quarter for stripes and appliqués

Rust: 1 fat quarter for stripes and appliqués

Batting: 16˝ × 54˝

Fusible adhesive (18˝ wide): ⅝ yard

CUTTING FABRICS

From Caramel:

Cut 2 rectangles 14½˝ × 28˝ for the backing.

Cut 1 strip 2½˝ × 32˝ for the stripes. Crosscut to make 2 strips 2½˝ × 16˝.

From Chocolate:

Cut 1 rectangle 14½˝ × 24½˝ for the top background.

From Merlot:

Cut 1 strip 2½˝ × 32˝ for the stripes. Crosscut to make 2 strips 2½˝ × 16˝.

Cut 4 strips 2½˝ × width of fabric for the binding.

From Moss:

Cut 4 strips 2½˝ × 16˝ for the stripes.

From Corn Silk:

Cut 4 strips 2½˝ × 16˝ for the stripes.

From Rust:

Cut 2 strips 2½˝ × 16˝ for the stripes.

ASSEMBLING THE RUNNER

1. Refer to the project photo (page 25) and illustration (page 29) as a guide, and stitch the long sides of the 2½˝-wide caramel, merlot, moss, corn silk, and rust strips together to create 2 striped blocks. Press toward the darker side as you finish stitching a seam. Square up and cut the blocks to make 2 striped blocks 14½˝ × 14½˝.

2. Stitch one of the sides of a block from Step 1 to one short end of the chocolate rectangle. Press the seam allowance to the chocolate side.

3. Repeat Step 2 to stitch the opposite side of the chocolate rectangle to one end of the other striped block. Flip the stripes like I did, if you like. Press toward the chocolate side.

4. To make the backing, stitch together 2 of the short ends of the caramel rectangles. Consider adding an inset as described in Backing Hints, page 8. See Creating the Appliqués (page 28) to continue.

place mats

FABRIC AND SUPPLIES

Note: A 42″ available width of fabric is assumed.

To make 2 place mats, 1 striped and 1 with stripes and circles:

Caramel: ⅝ yard for stripes, appliqués, and backing

Chocolate: 1 fat quarter for the top

Merlot: ⅝ yard for stripes, appliqués, and binding

Moss: 1 fat quarter for stripes and appliqués

Corn Silk: 1 fat quarter for stripes and appliqués

Rust: 1 fat quarter for stripes and appliqués

Batting: 2 pieces, each 16″ × 20″

Fusible web (18″ wide): ¼ yard

CUTTING FABRICS

From Caramel:

Cut 2 rectangles 16″ × 20″ for the backings.

Cut 1 strip 2½″ × 16″ and 1 strip 2½″ × 8″ for the stripes.

From Chocolate:

Cut 1 rectangle 14½″ × 12½″ for the top.

From Merlot:

Cut 2 strips 2½″ × 16″ and 1 strip 2½″ × 8″ for the stripes.

Cut 4 strips 2½″ × width of fabric for the binding.

From Moss:

Cut 3 strips 2½″ × 16″ and 2 strips 2½″ × 8″ for the stripes.

From Corn Silk:

Cut 2 strips 2½″ × 16″ and 2 strips 2½″ × 8″ for the stripes.

From Rust:

Cut 1 strip 2½″ × 16″ and 1 strip 2½″ × 8″ for the stripes.

ASSEMBLING THE PLACE MAT TOP

Place Mat with Circles & Stripes

1. Refer to the project photo (page 25) and illustration (page 29) as a guide, and stitch the long sides of the 2½″ × 8″ strips of caramel, merlot, moss, corn silk, and rust together to create a striped block. Press toward the darker side as you finish stitching a seam. Square up and trim the unit to make a striped block 6½″ × 14½″.

2. Stitch one long side of the block from Step 1 to one long end of the chocolate rectangle. Press the seam allowance to the chocolate side. See Creating the Appliqués (page 28) to continue.

Striped Place Mat

Refer to the project photo (page 25) and illustration (page 29) as a guide, and stitch the long sides of the 2½″ × 16 ″ strips of caramel, merlot, moss, corn silk, and rust together to create a striped block. Press toward the darker side as you finish stitching a seam. Square up and trim the unit to make a striped block 18½″ × 14½″. No appliqués are shown on this place mat, but feel free to improvise! See Quilting and Finishing (page 29) to continue.

table runner & place mats

CREATING THE APPLIQUÉS

All the appliqué template patterns are in the pullout section. They are all printed actual size. The blind-stitch appliqué method is used for the *Urban Vibe* projects. The appliqué templates are symmetrical and do not need to be reversed, so trace as many as you need directly onto freezer paper, and cut them out.

1. Place the freezer paper patterns onto the wrong side of the fabric, leaving ¼˝ around each piece. The plastic side of the freezer paper is up. Pin and cut around each piece, adding a ³⁄₁₆˝ seam allowance. Clip the curves.

2. With a hot, dry iron, carefully fold the fabric seam allowance over the edge of the freezer paper. Mini irons work well here!

POSITIONING AND STITCHING THE APPLIQUÉS

1. Refer to the project photos (page 25) and the illustrations (page 29) for placement. Arrange the appliqués on the background, overlapping the striped blocks and the quilt top edges as desired. Remember that there is a ¼˝-wide seam allowance for binding on all sides of the quilt top. Several of the circle appliqués extend into this seam allowance.

2. When you're satisfied with the arrangement of all of the appliqué pieces, pin them into place on the quilt top. Trim any excess fabric from the appliqué pieces even with the sides of the quilt top.

Blind-Stitch Appliqué

For the blind-stitch appliqué method used in this project, find the straight blind stitch on your sewing machine (often used for sewing hems). This stitch forms 4–7 straight stitches, then it forms a zigzag stitch to the left. Set both the stitch width and the stitch length very small. The width is narrow so it catches only two threads at the edge of the appliqué. The stitch length should be as low as you can handle comfortably.

Attach your open-toe or appliqué foot so you can easily see your work. To machine appliqué the pieces, I use a 60/8 universal needle with size .004 invisible monofilament quilting thread with bobbin thread to match either the backing or the background. Place the appliqué under the machine foot so that only the edge of the appliqué is caught in the zigzag and the straight stitches land right next to the appliqués, on the background. Stitch slowly so that you can follow the even curve of the circle appliqués.

More information on this blind-stitch appliqué method can be found in *Mastering Machine Appliqué*, by Harriet Hargrave. (See Resources, page 39).

3. Stitch around the circles, stopping about 2″ before you reach the beginning. Keeping the needle down in your fabric, remove the freezer paper.

4. Complete the stitching.

QUILTING AND FINISHING

Refer to Layering and Quilting (page 7) and Binding (page 9).

1. Sandwich the battings between the tops and the backing, wrong sides together, smoothing the tops outward from the center. Pin the layers together.

2. Quilt as desired. I used copper metallic thread on all three projects. For the runner and the circles and stripes place mat, I stitched a horizontal meandering pattern on the stripes, looping circles on the chocolate, and circular spirals in the circle appliqués. For the striped place mat, I used a horizontal meandering stitch pattern.

3. Bind the runner and placemats.

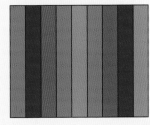

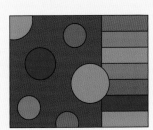

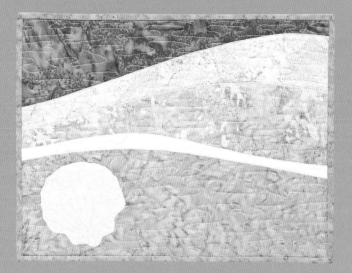

By the Sea

Graceful curves in colors of sea foam and sand create a pair of place mats that make great use of those batiks you've been collecting.

Finished size: about 14″ × 18″

Place mats made by Faith Kalback, Hope Kalback, Brenda Moseley, and Patrick

FABRIC AND SUPPLIES

Note: A 42″ available width of fabric is assumed.

To make 2 place mats, 1 with a sand dollar appliqué, and 1 with a scallop appliqué:

Light beige 1: ½ yard or 2 fat quarters for background

Light beige 2: 2 squares 6″ × 6″ for scallop and sand dollar appliqués

Dark beige: 1⅛ yards for appliqués, backing, and binding

Green: ¼ yard or 1 fat quarter for appliqués

Light teal: ¼ yard or 1 fat quarter for appliqués

Dark teal: ¼ yard or 1 fat quarter for appliqués

Batting: 2 pieces, each 16″ × 20″

Fusible adhesive (18″ wide): 1 yard

CUTTING FABRICS

From Light Beige 1:

Cut 2 rectangles 14″ × 18″ for the backgrounds.

From Dark Beige:

Cut 2 rectangles 16″ × 20″ for the backings.

Cut 4 strips 2½″ × width of fabric for the binding.

CREATING THE APPLIQUÉS

All the appliqué template patterns are in the pullout section. They are printed actual size and are reversed for tracing onto fusible web.

For this project, overlap the appliqué pieces as indicated on the illustrations on page 32.

Refer to Fusible Appliqué Preparations (page 7) for instructions on creating the appliqués.

POSITIONING AND FUSING THE APPLIQUÉS

1. Remove the paper backing from the appliqués.

2. Refer to the project photo (page 30) and illustration (page 32) for appliqué placement. The illustration shows the location of the template numbers in each place mat. Arrange the appliqués on the background fabric in the order shown, placing the sand dollar and the scallop last. Templates 1–4 are used in the scallop place mat, and templates 5–8 in the sand dollar place mat. Be sure to place the fusible side of the fabric against the background. Finger-press the appliqués into place. Remember that there is a ¼″-wide seam allowance on all sides of the background for the binding. The outer edges of templates 1–8 will extend into this seam allowance.

3. When you're satisfied with the arrangement of all of the appliqué pieces, fuse them into place on the background, following the manufacturer's instructions for the fusible web you're using.

QUILTING AND FINISHING

Refer to Layering and Quilting (page 7), Satin Stitching (page 8), and Binding (page 9).

1. Sandwich the batting between the place mat tops and their backings, wrong sides together, smoothing the place mat tops outward from the center. Pin the layers together.

2. Quilt as desired. I used a horizontal meandering quilting pattern across both tops, using a light beige thread color.

3. Satin stitch the edges of the appliqués. I used a light beige thread for this also.

4. Bind the place mats.

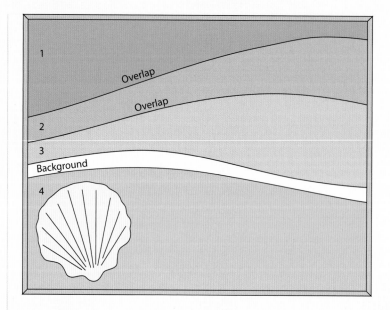

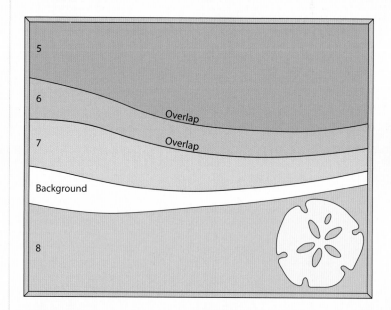

Starry & Striped

Here's a great runner for you to put together for your Independence Day gathering. You could easily scatter the stars on round or rectangular place mats to complete the table top.

Finished size: approximately 13½˝ × 52½˝

Table runner made by Gary Rushton and Patrick

FABRIC AND SUPPLIES

Note: A 42″ available width of fabric is assumed.

Navy: ¾ yard for star background and binding

Merlot: 1⅛ yards for stripes and backing

Ivory: ⅝ yard for star appliqués and stripes

Batting: 15″ × 54″

Fusible web (18″ wide): ½ yard

CUTTING FABRICS

From Navy:

Cut 1 rectangle 13″ × 13½″ for the star background.

Cut 4 strips 2½″ × width of fabric for the binding.

From Merlot:

Cut 7 strips 1½″ × width of fabric for the stripes. Remove the selvages.

Cut 2 rectangles 15″ × 28″ for the backing.

From Ivory:

Cut 6 strips 1½″ × width of fabric for the stripes. Remove the selvages.

ASSEMBLING THE RUNNER

1. Stitch the long sides of the 1½″-wide merlot and ivory strips together to create a striped block, beginning and ending with a merlot strip and alternating colors in between. Press toward the merlot side as you finish stitching a seam. Trim to straighten both ends, then cut the block in half, as the dashed line indicates.

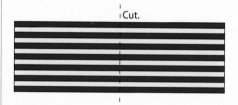

ı Cut.

2. Stitch one of the long sides of the 13″ × 13½″ navy rectangle to one short end of one of the striped blocks. Press the seam allowance to the navy side.

3. Referring to the project photo (page 33) and the illustration (page 35) for placement, repeat Step 2 to stitch the opposite side of the navy rectangle to one short end of the other striped block. Press toward the navy side.

4. For the backing, align one short end of each of the 15″ × 28″ merlot rectangles and stitch together. Consider adding an insert as described in Backing Hints, page 8.

CREATING THE APPLIQUÉS

All the appliqué template patterns are in the pullout section. They are printed actual size and are reversed for tracing onto fusible web.

Refer to Fusible Appliqué Preparations, page 7, for additional instructions on creating the appliqués.

POSITIONING AND FUSING THE APPLIQUÉS

1. Remove the paper backing from the appliqués.

2. Refer to the project photo (page 33) and the illustration to the right for placement. Remember that there is a ¼"-wide seam allowance for the binding on all sides of the runner top. Arrange the appliqués on the navy background, overlapping with the stripes and the edges as desired. Be sure to place the fusible side of the fabric against the background. Finger-press the appliqués into place.

3. When you're satisfied with the arrangement of all of the appliqué pieces, fuse them into place on the runner top, following the manufacturer's instructions for the fusible web you're using.

4. Trim excess appliqué fabric from the edges of the runner.

QUILTING AND FINISHING

Refer to Layering and Quilting (page 7), Satin Stitching (page 8), and Binding (page 9).

1. Sandwich the batting between the runner top and backing, wrong sides together, smoothing the quilt top outward from the center. Pin the layers together.

2. Quilt as desired. I used gold metallic thread in a large meandering quilting pattern, like that shown in Layering and Quilting (page 8), over the whole runner top.

3. Satin stitch around the star appliqués. I used gold metallic thread here also.

4. Bind the runner.

Hard Candy Christmas

Sparkling metallic thread, used for quilting and satin stitching, underscores the holiday cheer in a colorful Christmas candy runner.

Finished size: approximately 14˝ × 42˝

Table runner made by Gary Rushton and Patrick

FABRIC AND SUPPLIES

Note: A 42˝ available width of fabric is assumed.

Blue: 1 yard for background and backing

Red: ½ yard for candy cane appliqués and binding

White: ½ yard for round mint candy and candy cane appliqués

Green: 13˝ × 16˝ rectangle (or a fat quarter) for round mint candy appliqués

Batting: 16˝ × 44˝

Fusible web (18˝ wide): 1⅛ yards

CUTTING FABRICS

From Blue:

Cut 1 rectangle 14˝ × width of fabric for the background. Remove the selvages.

Cut 1 rectangle 16˝ × width of fabric for the backing. Remove the selvages.*

*Cut the backing in half, and add a coordinating inset to the backing as desired to make it larger than the background piece (see Backing Hints, page 8).

From Red:

Cut 4 strips 2½˝ × width of fabric for the binding.

CREATING THE APPLIQUÉS

All the appliqué template patterns are in the pullout section. They are printed actual size and are reversed for tracing onto fusible web.

Cut out the round mint candy appliqués and candy cane appliqués from white fabric. (Cut the complete candy cane shape.) Cut out the green fabric segments for the mint candies and the red segments (numbered 1–5) for the candy canes.

Refer to Fusible Appliqué Preparations (page 7) for additional instructions on creating the appliqués.

POSITIONING AND FUSING THE APPLIQUÉS

1. Remove the paper backing from the appliqués.

2. Refer to the project photo (page 36) and the illustration (page 38) for placement. Arrange the appliqués on the background, overlapping as desired. Place the green mint candy segments on top of the white circle appliqués, alternating with the white spaces. For the candy canes, place the red segments on top of the white appliqués as shown, alternating with the white spaces.

3. Be sure to place the fusible side of the fabric against the background. Finger-press the appliqués into place. Remember that there is a ¼˝-wide seam allowance for binding on all sides of the background. Two of the round mint candy appliqués and both candy canes extend into this seam allowance.

4. When you're satisfied with the arrangement of all of the appliqué pieces, fuse them into place on the background, following the manufacturer's instructions for the fusible web you're using. Trim the excess appliqué fabric from the sides of the runner.

QUILTING AND FINISHING

Refer to Layering and Quilting (page 7), Satin Stitching (page 8), and Binding (page 9).

1. Sandwich the batting between the runner top and backing, wrong sides together, smoothing the top outward from the center. Pin the layers together.

2. Quilt as desired. I used gold metallic thread in a looping circle pattern over the whole runner, including the appliqués.

3. Satin stitch around the outside of each appliqué as well as between all candy segments. I used green metallic thread for the round mint candy and red metallic thread for the candy canes.

4. Bind the runner.

ABOUT THE AUTHOR

Patrick has spent his professional years in a variety of creative fields. He began his career as an actor and singer, which eventually led him to designing costumes for stage and screen. Costuming credits include more than 50 productions and work with celebrities such as Liza Minnelli and Jane Seymour.

An artist and illustrator since childhood, Patrick works in many mediums. When he sits down to "doodle" at the drawing board, he never knows what one of his designs might become. But, whether it's designing quilts, wearable art, stationery products, or home decor, he enjoys creating it all.

A prolific designer, he is probably most well known for his very successful and long-running collections of fabric from Timeless Treasures and Moda that include his trademark marbleized solids, which are trendsetters in the industry. In order to be able to design in many fabric styles, he's chosen to work as a free agent, and his designs are currently with Robert Kaufman Fabrics, Timeless Treasures, and with Avlyn for Project Linus. Patrick's quilts, crafts, clothing, and home decorating accessories have appeared in such distinguished magazines as *Better Homes & Gardens, American Patchwork and Quilting, Country Crafts, Christmas Ideas, Halloween Tricks & Treats,* and many more. He has also written books on quilting and crafting for C&T Publishing and Sterling Publishing and has appeared on several television programs including *The Carol Duvall Show, Simply Quilts, Martha's Sewing Room, America Sews,* and, most recently, *America Quilts Creatively.*

RESOURCES

Patrick would like to thank the following companies and suggests them as great resources for quiltmaking materials:

FOR THREAD:
Sulky of America
www.sulky.com

FOR FABRIC:
Robert Kaufman Fabrics
www.robertkaufman.com

Timeless Treasures Fabrics, Inc.
www.ttfabrics.com

FOR LITE STEAM-A-SEAM 2 AND BATTING:
The Warm Company
www.warmcompany.com

NOTE: For complete information about machine appliqué, see *Mastering Machine Appliqué* by Harriet Hargrave, available from C&T Publishing.

Great Titles *from* C&T PUBLISHING

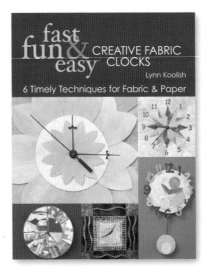

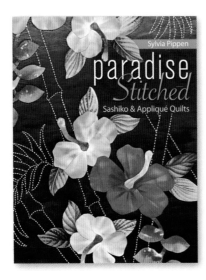
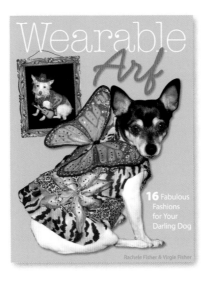
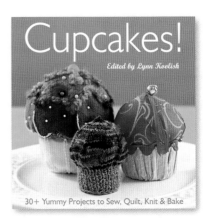

By the Sea
Make 1 from dark tea

By the Sea
Make 1 from light tea

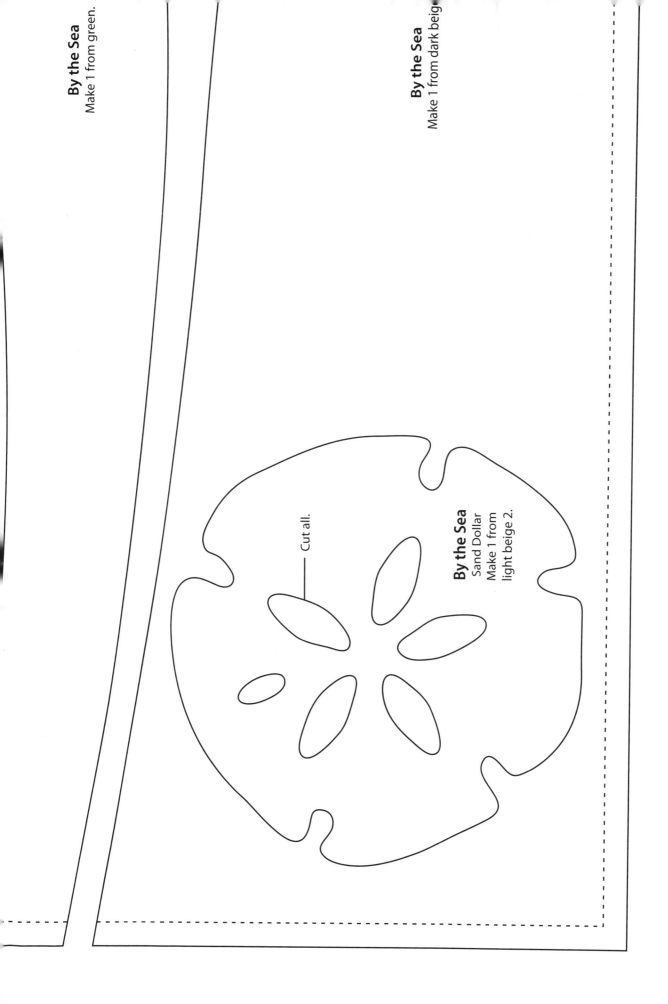

By the Sea
Make 1 from green.

By the Sea
Make 1 from dark beige.

Cut all.

By the Sea
Sand Dollar
Make 1 from
light beige 2.

P1

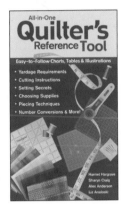

10 Quick & Easy Ways to Dress up a Table

- 10 fast, fun table toppers and placemats add charm to any table

- Super-easy fused appliqué designs

- Make a table runner, placemats, or a matching set of both

- Colorful designs for everyday, holidays, and special celebrations

- Simplified new appliqué techniques

- Full-size patterns

- Use a topper as a banner or brighten a bedroom by laying it across the foot of the bed

C&T PUBLISHING

10720

US $2

ISBN 978-1-57120-84

9 781571 208453

T4-BAN-211

NRAEF ManageFirst

Inventory and
Purchasing

Competency Guide

A Foundation Topic of the **NRAEF Certificate Program**

National Restaurant Association
EDUCATIONAL FOUNDATION

The National Restaurant Association Educational Foundation recognizes and thanks **American Express** as the Founding Partner of the new NRAEF ManageFirst Program™.

Together, we acknowledge the importance of educating tomorrow's restaurant and foodservice managers. The NRAEF ManageFirst Program is built on the management competencies that the industry believes are essential for success. The chart below outlines the NRAEF ManageFirst Program.

NRAEF ManageFirst Core Credential Topics

Competency Guide/Exam Topic	Associated Competencies
Hospitality and Restaurant Management ISBN 0-13-228380-8	■ Management practice ■ Leadership
Controlling Foodservice Costs ISBN 0-13-228336-0	■ Controlling foodservice costs
Human Resources Management and Supervision ISBN 0-13-222212-4	■ Shift management ■ Training and development ■ Staffing, hiring, recruiting and selection ■ Human resources administration and employee relations
ServSafe® Food Safety	■ Food safety and sanitation ■ Facilities and equipment management

NRAEF ManageFirst Foundation Topics

Competency Guide/Exam Topic	Associated Competencies
Managerial Accounting ISBN 0-13-228341-7	■ Managerial accounting ■ Budgeting
Inventory and Purchasing ISBN 0-13-222216-7	■ Inventory and purchasing
Customer Service ISBN 0-13-228381-6	■ Customer service
Food Production ISBN 0-13-175234-0	■ Food quality
Menu Marketing and Management ISBN 0-13-222201-9	■ Menu marketing and management
Restaurant Marketing ISBN 0-13-222206-X	■ Business promotions, marketing, and advertising
Nutrition ISBN 0-13-228386-7	■ Nutrition
ServSafe Alcohol™ Responsible Alcohol Service	■ Alcohol law and your responsibility ■ Recognizing and preventing intoxication ■ Checking identification ■ Handling difficult situations

To earn the credential, you must pass four core examinations and one foundation examination.